Battle Ready

Raintree OSPREY PUBLISHING

Civil War Union Troops

Philip Katcher • Illustrated by Ronald Volstad

This American edition first published in 2003 by Raintree, a division of
Reed Elsevier Inc., Chicago, Illinois, by arrangement with Osprey Publishing
Limited, Oxford, England.

For information, address the publisher:
Raintree, 100 N. LaSalle, Suite 1200, Chicago, IL 60602

First published 1986
Under the title *Men-at-Arms 177: American Civil War Armies (2) Union Troops*
By Osprey Publishing Limited, Elms Court, Chapel Way, Botley,
Oxford, OX2 9LP
© 1986 Osprey Publishing Limited
All rights reserved.

ISBN 1-4109-0119-X

03 04 05 06 07   10 9 8 7 6 5 4 3 2 1

Library of Congress Cataloging-in-Publication Data

Katcher, Philip R. N.
  [American Civil War armies. 2, Union troops]
  Civil War Union troops / Philip Katcher.
    p. cm. -- (Battle ready)
  Originally published: American Civil War armies. 2, Union troops. London
: Osprey, 1986, in series: Men-at-arms series.
  Summary: Looks at the uniforms and standard equipment of both soldiers
and officers of various regiments in the Union Army during the Civil
War.
  Includes bibliographical references and index.
  ISBN 1-4109-0119-X (library binding-hardcover)
  1. United States. Army--Uniforms--History--19th century--Juvenile
literature. 2. United States--History--Civil War, 1861-1865--Equipment
and supplies--Juvenile literature. [1. United States.
Army--Uniforms--History--19th century. 2. United States--History--Civil
War, 1861-1865--Equipment and supplies.] I. Title. II. Series.
  UC483.K43423 2003
  355.1'4'0973--dc21
                                    2003005642

Author: Philip Katcher
Illustrator: Ron Volstad
Editor: Martin Windrow
Printed in China through World Print Ltd.

Author's note
This book is designed to give the reader a brief but relatively comprehensive
guide to the uniforms, accoutrements, insignia, and weapons of the US Army's
three basic combat arms between 1861 and 1865.

  A good deal of emphasis will be found here on numbers and percentages.
The reason is that these figures do more to demonstrate what was actually
used or worn than do generalities. If we know that twice as many caps were
made as hats; and if we know that 75 percent of the men in a particular sample
wore caps; then we know that any modern historical reconstruction, from a
diorama to a living history display, should put more men in caps than hats.

  State names appear in regimental designations; yet most officers and
men in units, even those with state designations, wore and used the US
Army-issued uniforms, accoutrements, and weapons covered here.

CONTENTS

CIVIL WAR UNION TROOPS

INTRODUCTION

The US Army during the Civil War was the largest the country had raised in its brief history; and it would remain the largest ever raised until World War One. In all, 2,772,408 men served in some branch of the US Army during the Civil War; of these, 93,441 were blacks who served in combat units of US Colored Troops. Not all returned: 199,045 deserted (many to re-enlist under a different name for the bounty); 183,287 died of disease; 61,362 were killed in action, and 34,773 died later of wounds; 6,749 were posted as missing in action; 306 died of accidents, e.g. falling from trains; and 267 were executed for crimes such as desertion or murder.

The basic combat arms were the artillery, cavalry, and infantry. In all, 57 artillery regiments, 22 heavy artillery companies and 232 light artillery batteries were organized. There were 258 cavalry regiments, and another 170 independent cavalry companies. A total of 1,666 infantry regiments were raised, as were another 306 independent infantry companies.

The composition of each of these types of units was described in orders issued on May 1, 1861. A volunteer infantry regiment was to include ten companies, each with one captain; one first lieutenant, one second lieutenant, one first sergeant, four sergeants, eight corporals, two musicians, one wagoner, and between 64 and 82 privates. The regimental staff would comprise a colonel, a lieutenant-colonel, a major, a lieutenant to serve as adjutant, a chaplain, another lieutenant serving as a quartermaster, an assistant surgeon rated as a first lieutenant, a sergeant-major, a regimental quartermaster sergeant, a hospital steward, two principal musicians and 24 band members. (A regular army regiment differed in that it had two battalions, each with eight companies.)

A volunteer cavalry regiment was to have four, five, or six squadrons (while a regular cavalry regiment was to have three battalions, each with two squadrons). Two companies made up a squadron;

Despite the painted studio backdrop, this really is what the Union soldier looked like in the field. He wears, in this case, a plain forage cap; the "sack" coat with the collar turned up; and dark blue 1861 regulation trousers. His weapon is the M1842 .69-in, smoothbore musket. (David Scheinmann)

each company had a captain, a first lieutenant, a second lieutenant, a first sergeant, a company quartermaster-sergeant, four sergeants, eight corporals, two buglers, two farriers and blacksmiths, a saddler, a wagoner, and 56 privates. The regimental staff comprised a colonel, a lieutenant-colonel, a major, a lieutenant serving as an adjutant, a quartermaster, an assistant surgeon, a chaplain, a sergeant-major, a regimental quartermaster sergeant, a regimental commissary sergeant, a hospital steward, two principal musicians, and 16 band members.

An artillery regiment had 12 batteries, each consisting of a captain, one or two first lieutenants, one or two second lieutenants, a first sergeant, a company quartermaster sergeant, four to six sergeants, eight to 12 corporals, two musicians, two to six artificers, a wagoner, and between 58 and 122 privates. The regimental staff comprised a colonel, a lieutenant-colonel, three majors, an adjutant, a regimental quartermaster and commissary (a lieutenant), a chaplain, a quartermaster sergeant, a commissary sergeant, two principal musicians, a hospital steward, and 24 bandsmen.

(Bands were not mandatory; however, a survey made in October 1861 showed that 143 out of 200 regiments did have their own bands. The cost of a band was considerable, and in July 1862 it was ordered that all regimental bandsmen be discharged within 30 days. Thereafter, bands were confined to brigade or higher levels, or were made up of regular privates who did double duty as band members.)

According to orders of April 16, 1861, each brigade was to consist of four or more regiments, and each division, of two or more brigades.

The basic unit was, however, the individual in the ranks – the private. Although a larger percentage came from urban centers than was the case in the Southern army, he was usually a farmboy. In the great majority of cases, this was his first – and indeed only – major trip from the small town area from which he came. He considered himself, by the standards of the period, fairly well fed, paid, and equipped. His pay was $13 a month; although this was raised on May 1, 1864, to $16 a month, it was still considerably less than the $20 a month made by the average unskilled laborer in Connecticut just before the war. He received sufficient, albeit boring rations based on issues of salted meat and of the hard bread known as hardtack, but also including some attempts at providing more balanced nutrition. These included such items as desiccated vegetables – a compressed form of dried vegetables, largely turnips and peas, which expanded in water to make an almost edible soup.

His issued equipment was superior to that of his Confederate counterpart. It included a dress uniform consisting of a dress hat and dark blue

Hat and cap badges *top, left to right:* **artillery enlisted men; sidebadge for hat of all branches; cavalry enlisted men;** *bottom:* **infantry enlisted men. (Author's collection)**

frock coat or uniform jacket, and a fatigue blouse and cap. Both were worn with the same trousers. Initially, many of the issue uniform items were made of processed material called "shoddy." Gilbert Hays, 63rd Pennsylvania Volunteer Infantry, recalled: "Our first clothing was mostly miserable shoddy foisted on the government by rascally contractors. The trousers, as soon as they got wet, went to pieces, and nearly every soldier could be seen going around with his knees seeking the fresh air." Better wool clothes were issued after the first rush for uniforms of any description, although shoddy was a profitable product in wool mills and was used in making some clothing throughout the war. Black shoes known as "brogans" and sufficient underwear were included in the issue.

The soldier slung a cartridge box which held 60 rounds over his left shoulder and under his waistbelt, on which was hung his bayonet in its frogged scabbard, and a percussion cap box. From his right shoulder he slung his waterproofed haversack for rations, and a wool-covered tin canteen over that. His overcoat or blanket was carried in a waterproofed knapsack, or rolled with

Officers of the 2nd Delaware Infantry displaying variations in the use of corps badges. 1st Lt. Thomas Wenie, left, wears his II Corps trefoil on the top surface of his McClellan-style forage cap; the lieutenants next to him, and at right, wear their badges outlined in metallic braid on the sides of their slouch hats. The 2nd, or "Crazy Delawares," were the last unit to leave the field at Gaines' Mill, and the first to charge at both Fredericksburg and Gettysburg. (Author's collection)

an oilcloth or shelter-half to make up a blanket roll slung from left shoulder to right hip. His weapon was, if he were an infantryman, a single-shot rifled percussion lock musket, or a carbine, pistol, and saber if he were a cavalryman. Artillerymen were also issued swords for personal defense.

General orders of June 3, 1862, in the Army of Ohio specified that each man should carry only one blanket, two shirts, two pairs of underwear, two pairs of socks, one jacket or blouse, one pair of trousers, one pair of shoes, and one hat or cap. In November this was amended to allow each man a greatcoat, two flannel shirts, and a tin cup, plate, knife, fork, spoon, and towel.

Officers dressed generally as their men, with sabers hanging from their left hips and pistols carried on their right. In the field there was often little to differentiate them from the men they commanded.

It was not a dressy army. It did not appear to advantage on parade. But the men from whom it was drawn were down-to-earth types who came to do a job – save their country – rather than to stamp about parade grounds: and that, indeed, is what they did.

HEADGEAR

Both officers and men had two types of hats issued: a dress hat, and a fatigue cap.

Between May 1861 and October 1865 the Army bought 2,347,524 dress hats from contractors. These hats were officially made of black felt with a 6¼-in.-tall crown and a 3¼-in. brim, bound in black ribbed silk half an inch deep for officers, and made with a double row of stitching instead of this binding for enlisted men. In actual practice these hats, made by greedy contractors, were often considerably smaller than regulation, with crowns as short as 5½ in. and brims as narrow as 2¾ in. wide. (Many officers in fact preferred these smaller hats.) The brims were (officially) hooked up, on the left side (officially) for dismounted men and on the right for mounted, the hook concealed by a brass or embroidered eagle badge. Ostrich feathers – three for field grade officers, two for company grade, and one for enlisted men – were worn on the side of the hat opposite the hooked-up brim.

Besides the side badge, the hats were further decorated with hat cords – in mixed black and gold for officers and in branch-of-service-colored worsted for enlisted men – ending in two 2-in.-long tassels worn on the side of the hat opposite the feather. A gold lace band was worn around the base of the dress hats of the 2nd US Cavalry Regiment in 1861, apparently as a regimental distinction, which was unusual in the Army. On the front of the enlisted man s hat was a brass *Jäger* horn (bugle horn) for the infantry, crossed sabers, or crossed cannon, with a brass ⅝-in. regimental number and a 1-in. company letter above it. Officers wore the same basic insignia in gold embroidery, with a silver regimental number (but no company letter) above the cannon or sabers or within the loop of the infantry's horn.

This first lieutenant of the 6th New Jersey Inf. wears a commercially made metal version of the III Corps diamond badge suspended like a medal on his breast – a common practice, especially among officers. He also wears a black, military-style waistcoat, and a large watch chain. (Author's collection)

Generally, dress hats were unpopular. The 63rd Pennsylvania's Pte. Hays wrote: "The hats caused considerable grumbling among the boys. They were high, stiff affairs, and had enough brass fixings about them to make a copper kettle. We only wore them once, and were glad that they never asked us to wear them again." Pvt. Theodore Upson, 100th Indiana Infantry, wrote home in August 1861 that the men liked their uniforms "all except the hats. They are rediculous [sic] things, and make me think of the pictures of the Pigrim Fathers." Pvt. Henry Little, 7th New Hampshire Infantry, recalled that "the stiffening fairly got out of those old 'keg hats' until they lopped 'every which-way.'" Most men would have sympathized with the 111th Pennsylvania Infantry who, as they passed across the Shenandoah River in late 1861, tossed their dress hats into the flowing waters below the bridge.

Despite this, some Western regiments, including those of the Iron Brigade of the Army of the Potomac, wore their dress hats in the field, though often without any insignia or furniture. Indeed, a study of Western troops photographed in the field shows 12 percent of them wearing their dress hats as issued, although usually without any, or, at best, with very little in the way of insignia, feathers, or cords.

For dress occasions light artillery officers and men were to wear peaked shakos of the 1851–58 pattern, with red horsehair plumes, crossed cannon and eagle badges on the front, and worsted cords which passed around the shako and then down and across the soldier's back and chest. These were very rarely seen during the war, although 170 of them were sent to the 23rd New York Artillery in New Bern, North Carolina, in September 1863, and thereafter were stocked as a regular item by the Army. A slight variation of the light artillery shako appeared in 1864, but, again, was little used during the war. The Army purchased 15,738 of these shakos, in one form or another, made between May 1861 and October 1865. In June 1865, 154 of these were in New York, 1,500 in Boston, 744 in Philadelphia, and 1,000 were at Fort Monroe, Virginia.

The most popular cap was the issue forage, or fatigue cap. Besides making some 41,663 in their own depots, the US Army purchased 4,766,100 forage caps between May 1861 and October 1865. In a study of enlisted men photographed in the field with the Army of the Potomac between 1862 and 1865, 77.5 percent of infantrymen wore these caps, and 85 percent of the cavalrymen. A similar study of Western troops, notably less dressy than those from the East, showed that only 7.5 percent of them wore forage caps, and none of them had any sort of insignia on their caps at all.

These caps were made of dark blue wool with a stiff circular sheet of pasteboard forming the top surface, and were taller at the rear than the front, so that the crown inclined forward, French képi-style. The lining was of black or brown polished cotton, with a paper maker's label usually pasted to the inside of the top. The peak was of black glazed leather. Some peaks were horizontal, while others sloped down sharply over the wearer's eyes. Two small brass buttons secured a black glazed leather chinstrap, with a non-functioning brass sliding buckle usually worn in front. The chinstrap was adjustable so that it could be worn tight over the peak or under the chin.

In addition, each soldier was to receive once every four years a cap cover to be worn in foul

Col. Thomas Cass, 9th Massachusetts Inf., wears a typical field-grade officer's campaign dress. He has a loose-fitting plain blue "frock" with a single row of buttons, and white canvas and brown leather "sporting shoes." His saber is in a metal, rather than a leather-covered scabbard. Cass was one of 52 officers and men of the 9th Massachusetts who were killed at Gaines' Mill; another 147 were wounded, and 22 were posted missing. (Author's collection)

weather. These were of black oilcloth, and fitted over the top and sides of the forage cap, held in place by the chinstrap buttons. Between May 1861 and October 1865 the Army bought 674,586 cap covers from private suppliers. Obviously, not every cap had a matching cover; indeed, Pvt. Edward Harlan, 124th Pennsylvania Infantry, wrote in January 1863 that he and a friend made cap covers out of their rubber blankets. White linen or cotton havelocks, designed to prevent sunstroke, were also popular in 1861. These fitted over the cap like the

This New York officer wears the full dress of a company-grade officer, with its single row of buttons and its relatively thinner epaulet fringe. (Author's collection)

oilcloth cover, secured by the buttons, with a rear flap which covered the neck. One original example has a 12-in.-long flap extending between the two side buttons. According to John D. Billings, 10th Massachusetts Light Artillery: "if one of these articles survived active service three months I have yet to hear of it."

While not particularly attractive, the government issue caps were usually well made. Billings wrote that many soldiers of the Army of the Potomac in 1862 did not wear issue caps: "They bought the 'McClellan cap,' so called, at the hatters' instead, which in most cases faded out in a month. This the government caps did not do, with all their awkward appearance. They may have been coarse and unfashionable to the eye, but the colors would stand. Nearly every man embellished his cap with the number and letter of his company and regiment and the appropriate emblem (for his branch of service and/or corps)."

Many men did, indeed, so decorate their caps. It was regulation for company letters to be worn on the caps of enlisted men, and "the distinctive ornament of the corps and regiment in front" of those of officers. In addition, after March 1863 a system of colored cloth badges, usually worn on the hat or cap and indicating the wearer's corps and division, became official in many units. (These badges are covered in detail below.)

The infantrymen who did wear such badges appear, however, to have been largely those men serving in stationary posts. A study of photographs of infantrymen of the Army of the Potomac in the field indicates that 63.4 percent wore their caps with absolutely no decoration of any sort – corps badge, branch-of-service badge, regimental number, or company letter. Only 19.3 percent wore insignia – brass regimental numbers and/or branch-of-service horns, and sometimes cloth corps badges – on their caps. Another 18.2 percent wore only corps badges.

This was apparently a constant annoyance to senior officers, at least in the East. For example, one II Corps infantry regimental orderly book indicates in May 1863 that each man should wear a corps badge below a company letter and above the regimental number. Two weeks later, orders repeated that corps badges were to be worn on cap tops and "when soiled or lost they will be at once replaced." Apparently this did not happen, as similar orders appeared with some frequency, as in

A company officers' mess in the field. The officer at right wears enlisted men's sky blue trousers. (US Army Military History Institute)

February 1865, when orders stated that the corps badge should be worn along with "the letters, figures, and bugle." And on March 26, 1864, the following was noted in the orders of the 2nd Division, V Corps: "That in addition to the division badge, every man will be required to have on his cap the number of his regiment."

Mounted men, who showed a bit more pride in their branch, not surprisingly tended to wear cap badges. A study of enlisted cavalrymen of the Army of the Potomac photographed in the field between 1862 and 1865 indicates that 60 percent of them wore the crossed sabers insignia, often with company letters and regimental numbers.

Judging from photographs as well as from the quoted memoir of Pvt. Billings it appears that few men wore "McClellan" caps after 1862; but the same cannot be said for officers. Indeed, a study of period photographs shows about three McClellan caps being worn by officers for every two issue-style caps. The major difference between the two was that McClellan caps were cut with lower sides more like the true French képi of the period. Peaks were always flat, and usually had green undersides, with a thin leather binding the patent leather tops and the green undersides together.

These caps, also often known as "chasseur caps," were often worn by Zouaves (whose dress is covered in detail below). For example, the 72nd Pennsylvania Infantry wore sky blue chasseur caps with red piping around the outside of the crown and up all four sides. The 95th Pennsylvania Infantry wore the same cap but of dark blue. Officers of the 5th New York Infantry had these caps with dark blue bands and scarlet tops and sides, trimmed with gold braid. More commonly, however, Zouave enlisted men wore copies of the Algerian fez, with different colored tassels.

In much the same way, some non-Zouave officers also wore gold-trimmed caps. Maj. Henry O'Neill of the 118th Pennsylvania Infantry was described by the regiment's historian with a cap which "on the top and around the brim, was braided with rows of gold tinsel." This braid usually followed French Army style, with one line up the front, back and each side for lieutenants, two for captains, and three for field officers. The top surface usually bore a quatrefoil knot in the same number of braids.

Broad-brimmed, natural-colored straw hats were issued to the officers and men of the 16th New York Infantry in early 1862. Due to a fear that these made them stand out as targets, most of the straw hats were discarded during the Peninsular Campaign. A 22nd Massachusetts Infantry soldier recalled during that same campaign that in his unit, "some wore straw hats of every shape and color, others a black or

This New York first lieutenant wears a custom-tailored version of the fatigue sack coat, with pockets; the style of fastening only the top button of a coat or jacket was fashionable. Officers often wore coats like this instead of their frock coats when in the field. (Author's collection)

white slouch, while many sported a vizorless cap of that unique pattern so well remembered by all old soldiers, almost impossible to describe, which had increased the brown in their faces to a rich mahogany."

It is quite possible these latter were some type of pillbox cap. Col. Elisha Kellogg, 2nd Connecticut Heavy Artillery, was described as wearing such a cap during an attack on Cold Harbor in 1864. Such caps, apparently 3 to 3½ in. tall, appear in two photographs of officers of the 4th US Colored Infantry. A field grade officer wears a gold chin strap pushed up over the top of the crown, with an embroidered *Jäger* horn badge in front. A company grade officer has no chin strap, and wears a company letter on the front of his cap.

Often, in the field, enlisted men also wore non-regulation headdress. Chaplain H. P. Moyer, 17th Pennsylvania Cavalry, saw the men of his unit in a "great diversity of hats, straw hats, high shiny silk hats, old fashioned bell crowned hats, sun bonnets, and 'kiss me quicks,' the broad-brimmed plantation hats being largely in the majority." And Pvt. John Faller, 7th Pennsylvania Reserve Infantry, wrote home in December 1861 that Union artillerymen in Virginia were "running around with secesh [Confederate] hats." The broad-brimmed slouch hat was not typical in the East, but it was the most popular hat style among Western troops. Pte. Rice Bull, 123rd New York Infantry, wrote that Western troops "looked quite unlike our (Eastern) men... They all wore large hats instead of caps." Photographic evidence tends to bear this out, showing 82.7 percent of such troops in plain broad-brimmed felt hats, 13 percent of which were obviously civilian types sent from home. Others were cut-down dress hats: a 104th Illinois Infantry private spent one day, according to his diary, in which he "lowered the regulation felt hat, to a one-story affair" for members of his company.

Corps badges

Eventually a system of colored cloth badges became official wear, representing the wearer's corps and worn on the cap top, hat side, or left breast. These started with the "Kearny patch," adopted by Maj. Gen. Philip Kearny on June 27, 1862, to distinguish officers of his division from those of other divisions. No specific size, shape or material was ordered for the original Kearny patch: one 99th Pennsylvania

Officers of the 27th NY Light Artillery wearing the mounted officer's short jacket with the "Russian" shoulder knots prescribed for horse artillery officers. In the original photo a red braid quatrefoil knot can be made out on the top of the McClellan cap held by the man second from the right. (US Army Mil. Hist. Inst.)

Infantry soldier wrote in October that he wanted "a small star out of red flannel or any shape as you like best so I can sew it on my cap in memory of our late General Kearny." However, a 63rd Pennsylvania Infantry soldier recalled that "we were all allowed to wear the old Kearny badge, which is a square (1 in. x 1 in.) of deep red merino cloth."

In March 1863 this system of cloth badge identification became official in the Army of the Potomac. Each corps had its own shape of badge, and these came in red (for the corps' first division), white (for the second division), or blue (for the third division). Both dark and light blue were used for the third division badges: Pvt. Isaac Snively, 126th Pennsylvania Infantry, wrote in April 1863 that he wanted two dark blue and two light blue badges, and blue silk with which to sew them on.

The badges were: *I Corps*, a circle, adopted March 21,1863; *II Corps*, a trefoil (shaped like a stalked shamrock), adopted March 21, 1863; *III Corps*, a diamond or lozenge (the artillery dividing the diamond into four small diamonds and using the division color in the top and bottom diamond), adopted March 21, 1863; *IV Corps*, an equilateral triangle, adopted April 26, 1864; *V Corps*, a Maltese cross, adopted March 21, 1863; *VI Corps*, a Greek cross (with the St. Andrew's cross worn in the 1st and 2nd Divisions after April 19, 1864, and green badges worn in the Light Division), adopted March 21, 1863; *VII Corps*, a crescent encircling a star, adopted June 1, 1865; *VIII Corps*, a six-pointed star, never officially adopted but in use by July 16, 1864; *IX Corps*, a shield with a figure nine in the center, crossed with a fouled anchor and cannon (green worn in the 4th Division), adopted April 10, 1864; *X Corps*, a "four-bastioned fort" shape, adopted July 25, 1864; *Xl Corps*, a crescent, adopted March 21, 1863; *XII Corps*, a star, adopted March 21 1863; *XIII Corps*, no badge; *XIV Corps*, an acorn, adopted April 26, 1864; *XV Corps*, a cartridge box set transversely on a square with the motto "40 Rounds" (yellow

COATS

Officers' coats

Officers wore dark blue frock coats reaching down about two-thirds of the way between waist and knee, with a standing collar, three small buttons on each cuff, and pockets in the skirt folds. Field officers had two rows of seven buttons each, while company grade officers had one row of nine buttons. For dress occasions they wore gilt epaulets, with the branch-of-service indicated by a colored disc (red for artillery, yellow for cavalry, and sky blue for infantry) set on the crescent, with the regimental number embroidered on the disc in gold. The rank badges were worn on the epaulet strap, and included a silver eagle for a colonel; a silver leaf for a lieutenant-colonel; two silver bars for a captain, and a single bar for a first lieutenant. Field officers had ½-in. thick bullion epaulet fringes, while company grade officers had only ¼-in. thick fringes (hence the lack of need for a major's or a second lieutenant's insignia, these ranks wearing plain epaulets with the appropriate fringes).

In the field, officers wore transverse shoulder straps of the same branch-of-service color, 4 in. long by 1⅜ in. wide, with a ¼-in. gold embroidery round the edges, and the rank insignia set on each end. A colonel's eagle filled the entire strap; and a major was marked by a gold leaf at each end. In the Trans-Mississippi area officers were allowed to wear their rank insignia on the left breast instead of shoulder straps, embroidered on an approximately 2-in. diameter disc of branch-of-service color, edged with gold. In the field, generally, officers often simply pinned metal rank badges directly on to their shoulders or collars.

Mounted officers were also allowed to wear single- or double-breasted waist-length jackets, those of light artillery officers being marked by "Russian" shoulder knots with the rank insignia in silver on the outer, trefoil end. All officers not on duty could wear plain dark blue coats with regulation buttons. In fact, this became a common field dress, as officers bought and wore copies of the enlisted man's fatigue "sack" coat.

Enlisted men's coats

The enlisted foot soldier's dress coat was a frock coat like that worn by officers, but piped with branch-of-service color around the collar and on

Two infantrymen in regulation frock coats. At left, the enlisted man's dress hat worn in the regulation manner, although there should be a regimental number in the loop of the buglehorn. (Author's collection)

being worn in the 4th Division), adopted February 14, 1865; *XVI Corps*, a circle with four Minie balls, the points toward the cut-out center, not officially adopted; *XVII Corps*, an arrow, adopted February 26, 1865; *XVIII Corps*, a cross with foliate sides (yellow worn by unattached cavalry), to be worn on the left breast, adopted June 7, 1864; *XIX Corps*, a four-pointed star, adopted November 17, 1864; *XX Corps*, a star (green worn by the 4th Division), adopted April 26, 1864; *XXI Corps*, no badge; *XXII Corps*, a cinquefoil, adopted September 25, 1864; *XXIII Corps*, a heraldic shield, adopted September 25, 1864; *XXIV Corps*, a heart, adopted March 18, 1865; and *XXV Corps*, a square, adopted February 20, 1865.

This Massachusetts sergeant wears a common variation of the frock coat, with cuff piping parallel to the cuff edge instead of rising to a point – a variation often seen among troops from this state. Note the forage cap badges – the company letter "I" and the buglehorn of the infantry with a double-digit regimental number in the loop. (Author's' collection)

The most common dress coat variation of all is worn by this Connecticut corporal – a plain dark blue coat with no trim of any kind. (Author's collection)

the cuffs. There was one row of nine buttons down the front, and two small buttons on each cuff. Brass shoulder scales – made with rivets for regimental staff non-commissioned officers, slightly simpler for sergeants, and simpler yet for corporals and privates – were fixed to the dress coat. The government bought 1,881,727 foot dress coats between May 1861 and June 1865. Many men had company tailors lower their collars.

Mounted men wore a jacket which reached below the waistline, with a standing collar decorated with two false buttonholes. There were 12 small buttons down the front, two on each side of the collar, and two on each cuff. It was trimmed with branch-of-service color around all edges of the collar, the tops of the cuffs, down the front join, down back seams, and round the belt support pillars or rolls on the back. Shoulder scales were also worn with this jacket. The government also made jackets of rather skimpier design for economy reasons. These had only 11 buttons down the front, with cuffs that could not be unbuttoned, and a single row of lace making up each false buttonhole on the collar. Other dress jackets had shorter collars with only one false buttonhole. All told, the government bought 1,104,161 dress jackets between May 1861 and June 1865.

Musician Andy Kuher of Co. D, 150th Pennsylvania Vol. Inf., wears a dress coat with brass shoulder scales, and the framed bars of sky blue braid on the chest which marked an infantry musician. His cross belt supports, out of sight, a musician's sword. The 150th PA was one of the famous "Pennsylvania Bucktail" units, and Kuher's cap has the regimental distinction of a buck's tail attached to its side – note that this is a good deal bigger than it is often shown in reconstructions. Andy Kuher enlisted in August 1863, and died of illness in December the same year. (Ronn Palm)

The fatigue dress jacket was a "sack coat" made of dark blue flannel which reached half-way down the thigh, with an inside pocket on the left breast, and fastened with four coat buttons down the front. They came in four sizes: No. 1, 36-in. breast, 30½ in. long; No. 2, 38-in. breast, 31½ in. long; No. 3, 40-in. breast, 32½ in. long; and No. 4, 42-in. breast, 33fi in. long. The government bought 3,685,755 lined sack coats, which were, by regulation, for recruits only, and only 1,809,270 unlined sack coats, indicating that more men wore lined than unlined. The lining was usually a coarse, thin grey flannel in the coat body, with muslin sleeves. The government also bought another 530,144 "knit" sack coats. These coats were sometimes worn with the collars turned straight up, even fastened together with hooks and eyes sewn on them for that purpose.

In practice, in some units the dress coats were stored before taking the field, while in others the soldier had a choice of which coat to take. Photographs of groups of infantrymen of the Army of the Potomac in the field show that about 46 percent wore frock coats, while another 46 percent wore fatigue coats, with the rest wearing some form of waist-length jacket. Plain dark blue jackets with standing collars and nine brass buttons down the front appear to have been a commonly issued item by 1864, a large number of veterans being photographed in such jackets. Of cavalrymen, however, only 43 percent wore their dress jackets in the field.

Non-commissioned grades were indicated by chevrons worn points down on both sleeves above the coat elbows. The grades were: sergeant major, three bars and arcs; quartermaster sergeant, three bars and straight "ties" (three bars and one tie seems to mark a company quartermaster sergeant after 1863, although not officially until 1866); first sergeant, three bars and a lozenge; sergeant, three bars; corporal, two bars; and a pioneer, crossed hatchets with 4½-in. long handles and 2-in. long blades. Cavalry saddlers appear to have worn yellow cloth saddle knives as unofficial sleeve badges. Veterans were marked by branch-of-service color half-chevrons (diagonal bars) ½ in. wide, worn below the elbow, starting a ½ in. above the cuff trim, and extending from seam to seam, low at the front and high at the back. Service in war was marked by red edges (sky blue in the artillery). These service stripes were only to be worn on dress coats.

Cpl. Windsor B. Smith of the 1st Maine Cav. wears a common variation on the mounted man's jacket, with only one false buttonhole loop on the lower collar. The jacket bears regulation yellow braid trim, but as so often in this period, it has photographed black. Smith was captured by the Confederates near the Weldon Railroad in September 1864; he was exchanged in April 1865, but his health was broken, and he never returned to active duty. (Author's collection)

Unusually clear portrait of a company quartermaster sergeant wearing the regulation mounted man's short jacket. A prominent seam up the inside of the legs shows the doubled reinforcement added to the trousers of mounted personnel. (Rick Carlile)

Buttons

Buttons on shirts and trousers were tinned iron, made with four holes for attachment to the garment. The officers' coat and waistcoat buttons, however, were, according to 1855 orders, "gilt, convex, device a spread eagle with the letter A, for Artillery, I, for Infantry, R, for Riflemen, C, for Cavalry, D, for Dragoons, on the shield; large size, ⅞ in. external diameter; small size, ½ in.

"For all enlisted men – yellow, the same as used by the Artillery, &c.; omitting the letter in the shield."

Vests

Officers were allowed to wear buff, white, or blue vests. In fact, these were worn by both officers and enlisted men, especially in cooler weather or while stationed in fixed locations. They actually came in both dark and sky blue – white or buff were rarely seen – made with a standing collar, and three or four slash pockets in front. One original sky blue vest is made of a cotton-wool mixture cloth similar to, but much lighter than, the uniform trousers. Most vests were probably made of this lighter cloth. The backs were of dark brown or black polished cotton, with a belt and buckle across the rear of the waist for size adjustment. The small brass buttons bore the eagle and, in the case of officers, branch-of-service initial letters. The Army

This regimental quartermaster sergeant wears the plain blue jacket so often seen among veterans; note the service stripe on his forearms, He holds a non-commissioned officer's sword. (Author's collection)

purchased around 10,000 of them, apparently to be sold to officers or men.

Most vests came from home. Sgt. Maj. Lucius Shattuck, 24th Michigan Infantry, wrote home in January 1863 that he wanted a "military vest of black cloth, single-breasted, buttoning to the chin." From photographs of Army of the Potomac enlisted men, taken between 1862 and 1864, it appears some 22 percent wore vests, mostly in the colder months.

OTHER UNIFORM ITEMS

Shirts
Between May 1861 and October 1865 the Army purchased 11,091,639 shirts. They also bought 5,532,729 yards of Canton flannel (cotton) and 8,314,892 of grey cloth, apparently mostly for making shirts. The Quartermaster described the shirts as being "Zouave, gray," knit, and flannel. The flannel shirts were mostly grey. General orders in the Army of Tennessee in April 1862 pointed out that "the regiments today went out in gray flannel shirts, which at a distance of 100 yards resembles the seccession uniform. Commanders of regiments must never leave their camps for action unless the men wear the blue coat, jacket or blouse."

An original issue shirt in a private collection is made of heavy unbleached muslin. It has a two-piece collar with a tin button on one side and a button-hole on the other. Made in pullover style, it has no other buttons down the front. The cuffs were made by simply turning back the sleeves and sewing them down, with one tin button fastening each cuff. There are no pockets. It has an inspector's mark and date on the rear shirt tail about an inch from the hem.

A 22nd Massachusetts private in November 1862 drew "a shirt (white cotton and wool shoddy, no shape or make)" and Pvt. Upson of the 100th Indiana wrote that issue shirts were "rather coarse and scratchy." Civilian shirts were also worn. Pvt. William Margraff, 6th Pennsylvania Reserves, wrote home in June 1861 for "a couple of striped shirts and a fine shirt," and one officer noted that sutlers did well after the Battle of Antietam because the men "were willing to pay any price demanded for shirts."

Ties
The Army bought 745,814 leather stocks between May 1861 and October 1865. Few were actually issued, and even fewer, apparently, were worn. They were of black leather, 2 in. wide, curved to dip under the chin, 13⅓ in. long, with a 4½-in. long thin leather strap ⁹⁄₁₀-in. wide mounted at one end fastened by a 1-in. waistcoat buckle at the other. There was a tooled line around the outer edge of the stock. Officers were permitted to wear ties, but these were not allowed to show at the collar opening.

Undershirts
Pvt. Leo Faller of the 7th Pennsylvania Reserves wrote home in October 1862 that he had drawn "brown knit undershirts." From photographs these appear to have no collar or cuffs, to be made of tan material, with one button on the neckband, and two

more down a placket that stops about 4 in. above the navel. They were made in pullover-style.

Trousers

According to 1861 regulations, trousers were dark blue with, for regimental officers, "a welt let in the outer seam, one-eighth of an inch in diameter, of colors corresponding to the facings...." Enlisted men had dark blue trousers, with branch-of-service color stripes 1½ in. wide for sergeants and ½ in. wide for corporals. Photographs suggest that over half the non-commissioned officers in the field did not bother to put stripes on their trousers – these were

This saddler wears the fatigue sack coat with mounted man's trousers. His unofficial saddler's badge is worn on both sleeves just above the elbows. His spurred riding boots are worn inside the trousers. (Rick Carlile)

This private, identified as John B. Nick of the 2nd District of Columbia Inf. Regt., wears a custom-made version of the sack coat: these were often seen among veterans, sometimes almost to the length of a frock coat. He wears a dark blue military-style waistcoat, and his low, fairly small-brimmed black slouch hat is seen on the table. The regiment was part of the V Corps of the Army of the Potomac. (Author's collection)

not issued already made up with stripes. The trouser color was officially changed from dark to sky blue December 16, 1861, with dark blue stripes for infantry non-commissioned officers. These trousers were dyed sky blue, a color which acquired a somewhat greenish cast after several washings. Mounted men also had a second layer of wool sewn as reinforcement inside the legs and under the crotch. The Army bought 6,068,049 pairs of foot soldiers' trousers and 1,688,746 pairs for mounted men between May 1861 and October 1865.

the 100th Indiana recalled drawing his first issue in 1861: "The drawers are made of Canton flannel. Most of the boys had never worn underwear and they did not know what they were for and some of the old soldiers who are here told them they were for an extra uniform to be worn on parade and they half believed it." The underwear, of a tan color, were made two-thirds of the leg length, with several buttons on the waistband and down the fly.

Gaiters

Gaiters were not a regulation part of the uniform, although the Quartermaster General wished them to be regulation for the infantry as early as 1860. Many units appear to have drawn and worn them,

This is apparently a member of the US Sharpshooters; he holds a breech-loading Sharps rifle. Note his issue undershirt, and long canvas gaiters. (Rick Carlile)

A second lieutenant wearing the officer's overcoat, with its wrist-length cape and four black frogs and toggles fastening across the chest. This particular rank is indicated by the lack of sleeve rank insignia. (Author's collection)

Trousers came with five tin fly buttons and four buttons around the waist for braces (which were not issued). Sometimes there was a belt let into the rear for size adjustment; but most had simply a slit in the rear, with two holes through which a piece of twine or rawhide was tied for size adjustment. Pockets were either cut straight or made with flaps. A watch pocket on the right waistband was usually included. A private in the 104th Illinois wrote that he had converted "the old style pants pockets to square styles" for friends in his company.

Underwear

Between May 1861 and October 1865 the Army purchased 10,738,365 pairs of underwear. Upson of however, and not only the Zouave units which received them as a standard part of their uniform. Photographs of the 110th Pennsylvania Infantry in spring 1863 show gaiters to have been worn, even though the regiment's uniforms were unremarkable in all other respects. Pvt. Leo Faller, 7th Pennsylvania Reserves, wrote that he drew a "pair of white leggings" on May 24, 1862. And Confederate General John Gordon described a Union attack at Antietam: "The entire force, I concluded, was composed of fresh troops from Washington or some camp of instruction. So far as I could see, every soldier wore white gaiters around his ankles." The troops in this attack – the 5th Maryland, 1st Delaware, and 4th New York Infantry Regiments – had, indeed, been stationed around Washington before the battle.

An original pair, worn by a member of the 114th Pennsylvania Infantry, are made of heavy white linen, 10¼-ins high, with six tin buttons down the outside. A 1½-in. black leather strap is fixed with copper rivets inside, and passes under the instep to fasten to the outside bottom button.

Shoes

The infantryman's issue shoe was an ankle-high laced shoe, often made with the rougher flesh side of the black leather on the outside. Soles came both pegged and sewn. In all, the Army bought 1,468,548 pairs of sewn-sole shoes and 1,073,066 pairs with pegged soles. Each man was supposed to receive four pairs of shoes a year, although mounted men could get two pairs of boots instead of shoes. These boots reached mid-calf; some 70 percent of photographed cavalrymen wear them under their trousers, instead of tucking the trousers into the boots.

Pvt. William Margraff, 6th Pennsylvania Reserves, wrote home in November 1861: "A pair of good boots is something that we can't get along without... Uncle Sam doesn't furnish us anything but shoes to wear in the winter. The shoes are very good ones to wear in the summer, as they are made with the best of leather, and are made by the best of shoemakers." The 7th Pennsylvania's Pvt. Faller agreed about the value of the boots over shoes, as the former, he wrote in November 1861, "will be a great deal warmer." But a number of soldiers disagreed with Margraff about the quality of the issue shoe. Gen. Samuel Curtis wrote in February 1862: "I find the men's shoes so miserable, they have worn them

Col. J. Barrett Swain, 11th NY Cav., wears a fleece-trimmed frogged jacket instead of an overcoat; this European-style garment was popular among mounted officers. Swain was apparently a poor officer, his absence "in quarters, ill" often being noted when the unit went into action. He was dismissed in February 1864. (Benedict R. Maryniak)

entirely out in six days' marching." Lt. Moses Osmay, 104th Illinois Infantry, went further, writing: "The shoes found by the government are often miserable frauds," and a 22nd Massachusetts infantryman wrote that he had been issued "flimsey paper-soled contract brogans."

Many officers and men preferred, at least in summer, to buy light-weight, combination white canvas and brown leather "sporting shoes." These had leather toes, ties, heels, and soles. At times these were even issued – Margraff of the 6th Pennsylvania recalled receiving "a pair of nice white shoes" in July 1861 – but more often they came from sutlers or from home.

Socks

The Army bought 20,319,896 pairs of grey or tan woolen socks during the Civil War. Billings recalled: "There was little attempt to repair the socks drawn from government supplies, for they were generally of the shoddiest description, and not worth it. In

symmetry, they were like an elbow of a stove-pipe; nor did the likeness end there, for while the stove-pipe is open at both ends, so were the socks within forty-eight hours after putting them on."

Socks were often used for gaiters. Pvt. Robert Strong, 105th Illinois Regiment, recalled: "For days we would march with our pants stuck in our stockings and the stockings held up by strings, with mud coming over the top of our shoes at every step."

Overcoats

Commissioned officers wore dark blue overcoats with four black silk frogs across the chest, a detachable cape which reached down to the coat cuffs, and black silk braid on each cuff indicating rank. The number of braids ran from five for a colonel to one for a first lieutenant; second lieutenants wore no braid.

This infantry private wears a dark blue version of the foot soldier's overcoat, as issued in 1861; and the side badge from the dress hat is pinned to the front of his forage cap. (David Scheinmann)

A dashing figure, with dashing whiskers, adopts a dashing pose! He wears the regulation mounted man's double-breasted caped overcoat, and a dress hat worn brim-down and without insignia. (Rick Carlile)

The foot enlisted man had a sky blue wool coat with a standing collar, a single row of five buttons, and an elbow-length cape that fastened with six buttons. The mounted soldier's coat differed only in that it had a laydown collar, two rows of buttons on the front, and a cape that reached the cuffs. Between May 1861 and October 1865 the Army bought 2,803,519 foot soldiers' overcoats, 1,023,531 mounted soldiers' overcoats, and 34,710 "talmas." A talma was a rubber- or gutta percha-coated coat with sleeves that reached to the knee, which was supposed to be issued to the cavalry; it lacked a cape, and was worn over the overcoat. Talmas were not issued after 1862, when cavalrymen received ponchos in their place.

Because of the desperate rush to get men clad, in October 1861 the Army issued dark blue, black, and even (among Ohio troops) brown overcoats as well as sky blue ones. From late 1861 officers were allowed to wear enlisted men's overcoats "in time of actual field service" to make themselves less visible.

Overcoats were not always popular. A cannoneer with Lilly's Indiana Battery wrote home in 1864 that he did not use an overcoat since "it is more trouble than it is worth in rainy weather. A rubber poncho will keep me dry and does not tire me to death to carry it and in cold weather they do not do such a powerful sight of good in keeping one warm for they are split so far up the back that they let the cold in on the rear, and do but little good on the shoulder." Another artilleryman solved this problem by lining his coat cape with rubber blanket material, "so that on unbuttoning it off the collar and turning it wrong side out it became water proof."

Sashes

Regimental officers were to wear crimson silk net sashes with silk bullion fringed ends, passed twice around the waist and tied behind the left hip, the pendant part hanging no more than 18 in. below the tie. First sergeants and above had red worsted sashes with worsted bullion fringe ends, worn in exactly the same manner. The Army purchased 25,717 sergeants' sashes between May 1861 and October 1865. Sashes were supposed to be worn on all occasions except for stable and fatigue duties, but were actually rarely worn in the field. In addition, the "officer of the day" was marked by wearing a sash across his body from right shoulder to left hip instead of around his waist.

ZOUAVE AND CHASSEUR UNIFORMS

In September 1861 the Army ordered 10,000 sets of complete uniforms and accoutrements for French Army *chasseurs à pied de la ligne* to be shipped the following month. The shipment included tents and knapsacks, but no officers' equipment. The chasseur coat was a short dark blue frock with slits in the skirt sides, piped yellow, and with fringed worsted epaulets. The trousers were blue-grey, and

Although regulations called for chevrons to be worn above the elbow, the overcoat cape would have hidden them, so most NCOs wore them above the overcoat cuff – as does this first sergeant of New York cavalry. Note, too, his scarlet NCO's sash; and the very large size of the diamond above the chevrons in his rank insignia. Neither the gloves nor the high boots were issue items. (Rick Carlile)

ZOUAVE REGIMENTS

The following regiments were, at some point in their existence, completely equipped with Zouave type uniforms. There were also some individual companies of regiments – e.g. such as Co. K, 19th Massachusetts Infantry, or Co. K, 69th Pennsylvania Infantry – who wore Zouave uniforms for periods of time; however, these companies seldom maintained their unique uniforms beyond the initial issue. There were also regiments, mostly from the West, who wore semi-Zouave jackets, but no other particular Zouave dress: these are not listed here.

Unit	Cap	Jacket	Vest	Shirt	Trim	Sash	Trousers
11th Indiana (first uniform)	Grey képi, red crown	Grey	—	Light blue, grey	Red, sky blue	—	Grey
(second uniform)	Blue forage	Black	Dark blue, false		Light blue	—	Sky blue
33rd New Jersey	Blue képi, red trim	Dark blue	Dark blue	—	Red, light blue	Dark, light blue binding	Dark blue
35th New Jersey	Blue fez, yellow tassel	Dark blue	Dark blue	—	Red, light blue	Dark, light blue binding	Dark blue
3rd New York	Scarlet fez, blue tassel	Dark blue	Dark blue	—	Magenta	Turquoise	Dark blue
5th New York	Scarlet fez, blue, yellow tassels	Dark blue	Medium blue	—	Medium blue	Red, light blue edging	Scarlet
9th New York	Scarlet fez, blue tassel	Dark blue	Dark blue	—	Magenta	Turquoise	Dark blue
10th New York	Red fez	Dark brown	Scarlet	—	Red	Sky blue, red edging	Sky blue, red stripes
11th New York	Red fez	Dark blue	Dark blue	—	Red	Blue	Dark blue
17th New York	Scarlet fez, blue tassel	Dark blue	Dark blue	—	Magenta	Turquoise	Dark blue
44th New York	Blue forage	Dark blue	—	—	Red	—	Dark blue

the uniform included gaiters. These uniforms were issued as a reward for proficiency in drill to the 18th Massachusetts Infantry, 62nd and 83rd Pennsylvania Infantry, and 49th and 72nd New York Infantry Regiments, among others.

Many other units also chose to dress themselves in copies of French Zouave uniform, made fashionable by the exploits of such regiments in the 1850s in the Crimea and Italy. These originally included dark blue short jackets trimmed with red tape, a dark blue vest trimmed red, very baggy red trousers, leather-bound gaiters, and a red fez with a dark blue tassel, partly covered by a separate turban. Very few American units wore accurate copies of the authentic Zouave dress. Most made the trousers narrower than the true Arab *seroual*; many had false vest fronts permanently attached to the front opening of the jackets; some simply altered issue jackets with Zouave-like trim, but otherwise wore issue dress. In some units only one company was turned out in Zouave dress – something which rarely lasted long. Still, there were units dressed in some version of the Zouave uniform throughout the war, and present at virtually every major battle.

The *vivandière*, a female sutleress tricked out in a form of military dress who accompanied the troops, was another French innovation popular with many Zouave and Chasseur units. One soldier of the 99th Pennsylvania Infantry wrote home that "John Witherson's wife" was "dressed in the same manner that the boys of the 23rd Pa. Regiment [sic]. At a distance you could hardly tell them from boys. They had just the same as men do ownley [sic] I did

Unit	Cap	Jacket	Vest	Shirt	Trim	Sash	Trousers
53rd New York	Red fez, yellow tassel	Dark blue	Dark blue	—	Yellow	Sky blue	Sky blue
62nd New York	Red fez, blue tassel	Dark blue	Dark blue	—	Deep red	Blue	Sky blue
74th New York	Red fez, blue tassel	Dark blue	Dark blue	—	Yellow	Light blue	Red
140th New York	Red fez edged yellow, dark blue tassel	Dark blue	Dark blue	—	Red	Dark blue bound red	Sky blue
146th New York	Red fez, red tassel	Sky blue	Sky blue	—	Yellow	Red	Sky blue
164th New York	Dark blue képi	Dark blue	Dark blue	—	Dark red	Turquoise	Dark blue
165th New York	Scarlet fez, blue tassel	Dark blue	Medium blue	—	Medium blue	Red edged light blue	Scarlet
34th Ohio	Red fez	Dark blue	Dark blue	Red	Red	—	Sky blue, 2 red stripes
23rd Pennsylvania	Blue forage cap	Dark blue	Dark blue	—	Red	—	Dark blue, piped red
72nd Pennsylvania	Sky blue képi trimmed red	Dark blue	None	—	Red	None	Sky blue, red stripe
76th Pennsylvania	Dark blue fez, dark blue tassel	Dark blue	Grey	White	Magenta	Red	Medium blue
91st Pennsylvania	Red fez	Dark blue	Dark blue	—	Yellow	—	Sky blue
95th Pennsylvania	Blue képi trimmed red	Dark blue	None	Blue	Red trimmed red	—	Sky blue
114th Pennsylvania	Red fez, yellow tassel	Dark blue, sky blue cuffs	Dark blue	—	Red	Light blue	Red
155th Pennsylvania	Red fez, blue tassel	Dark blue	Dark blue	—	Yellow	Red edged yellow	Dark blue piped red

not see their revolvers." Another *vivandière* was described by a 27th Pennsylvania infantryman: "She wore a blue zouave jacket, a short skirt trimmed with red braid, which reached to just below her knees, and trousers over a pair of boots. She wore a men's sailor hat turned down." Eliza Wilson of the 5th Wisconsin Regiment was described in 1862: "She dresses in clothes of such pattern as the military board have ordered for nurses in the army, which is the Turkish costume. The color is bright brown; no crinoline; dress reaches halfway between the knee and ankle; upper sleeve loose, gathered at the wrist; pantalettes same color, wide but gathered tight around the ankle, black hat with plumes, feet dressed in Morocco boots."

ACCOUTREMENTS

Beltplates

The infantryman's oval brass lead-backed waist beltplate was 3.5 in. long by 2.225 in. wide, bearing the letters "US" within a raised oval border on the front. There were two studs and a hook of brass embedded in the lead on the back. Between January 1, 1861, and June 30, 1866, the Army bought 143,348 of these plates.

The infantryman's shoulder beltplate was also of stamped brass, lead-backed; it was circular, 2½ in. in diameter, with two iron wire loops on the back which slid through slits in the shoulder belt and were fastened by inserting a strip of rawhide. The design showed the national eagle clutching a sprig of laurel and a bundle of arrows. The same plate was worn on the NCO's sword belt. (In fact, at least three soldiers were photographed wearing the shoulder beltplate on their waist belts.) The Army bought 151,573 of these plates, and, despite their uselessness, 70 percent of the infantrymen of the Army of the Potomac photographed in the field between 1862 and 1865 are wearing them.

The plate worn by officers, non-commissioned officers, and all mounted men was rectangular, 3½ in. long and 2.2 in. wide. Of cast brass, it bore the design of an eagle surrounded by a wreath, the wreath being made of German silver; it had a slot at one end through which the belt was passed. The Army bought 44,275 of these plates; many more were privately made and sold directly to officers.

Belts

The issue infantry waist belt was of black leather, 1.9in. wide and 38.5 in. long, with a leather loop or a strip of sheet brass bent around to form loops at the end.

A sergeant-major wearing the French Chasseur uniform issued to a number of regiments in the Army of the Potomac, and holding an NCO's sword. Note the *brides* for attaching epaulets at the point of the shoulder; and the French *bonnet de police*, complete with tassel, worn here askew with the "front" above the outer corner of his left eye. (Michael J. McAfee)

Officers in Zouave units generally wore regulation dress with only slight differences; for instance, they often wore red trousers of conventional cut if their men were in red Zouave trousers. Caps were usually decorated in the French manner, as in this photograph of a captain: with braid piping around the band, vertically up the four sides, around the crown, and in a quatrefoil knot on the top surface. Note also the buttoned tabs on the coat to secure the sword belt in place. (David Scheinmann)

1: Colonel, Infantry, 1861
2: Sergeant major, Infantry, 1861
3: 1st Lt., Infantry, 1861

3

1

2

A

1: Lt. Col., Cavalry, 1863
2: Sergeant, Cavalry, 1863
3: Captain, Cavalry, 1863

VOLSTAD

B

1: Captain, Light Artillery, 1864
2: Corporal, Light Artillery, 1864
3: Regt. QMS, Heavy Artillery, 1864

C

1: Private, Infantry, 1863
2: 2nd Lt., Infantry, 1863
3: 1st Sgt., Infantry, 1863

D

1: Co. QMS, Cavalry, 1864
2: Private, Infantry, 1864
3: Musician, Cavalry, 1864

2

1

3

E

1: Private, Infantry, 1862
2: Private, 35th NJ Vol. Inf., 1864
3: Private, 5th NY Vol. Inf., 1863

F

1: Private, 155th PA Vol. Inf., 1864
2: Captain, 155th PA Vol. Inf., 1864
3: Private, 3rd Div., XIII Corps, 1864

1: Musician, 3rd Div., II Corps, 1865
2: Private, Light Artillery, 1865
3: Major, Artillery 1865

H

Belts were made of both bridle and buff leather. Between January 1, 1861, and June 30, 1866, the Army bought or made 44,275 of these belts, in addition to 2,065,875 sets of complete infantry accoutrements.

The sergeant's and musician's waist belt was 36 to 40 in. long and 1.9 in. wide, with at one end a brass hook fastened with three brass wire rivets, and at the other a brass loop which connected to the beltplate. The Army bought or made 9,598, clearly insufficient for every NCO: not surprisingly, many were photographed in the private's belt.

The non-commissioned officer's sword belt was worn over the right shoulder to the left hip. It was of black buff leather, 2.3 in. wide; the short section (i.e. that worn between the plate and the left hip frog) was 17 in. long, and the long section that passed up the back and over the shoulder, 40 in. long. It had a leather loop in front; and a frog with two sections, for the bayonet scabbard and the sword. The Army made or bought 20,957 of these belts.

The saber belt was of black buff leather (sometimes bridle leather) between 36 and 40 in. long. It was 1.9 in. wide, with a square loop for attaching the slings and the shoulder strap. A brass hook was riveted on one end by three brass wire

Photographed in abandoned Confederate works near Centerville, Virginia, in March 1862, these dimly-seen soldiers appear from their silhouettes to include some Zouaves, quite possibly from the 23rd Pennsylvania Volunteers. The figures at right wear baggy dark blue trousers, brown canvas gaiters, short dark blue jackets with a row of buttons up each side of the front, and ordinary forage caps. Note so-called "Quaker cannon" – propped-up logs, used by the Confederates during their occupation of these positions to fool the enemy into overestimating their artillery strength. (US Army Mil. Hist. Inst.)

rivets, and a cast brass loop was sewn on the other end to connect with the plate. The 40-in. shoulder strap was 1.125 in. wide, and had two brass hooks to attach to the belt. There were two saber slings, the front one 17 in. long and the rear one 34 in. long. There was a brass saber hook, from which the saber was hung when dismounted, next to the front sling on the left hip. The Army made or bought 304,365 of these belts for cavalrymen and another 73,139 for horse artillerymen, plus 196,351 complete sets of cavalry accoutrements.

The foot artilleryman's buff leather sword belt was made in three pieces, all 1.9 in. wide, connected together by two brass loops. There was a frog on the left suspended to the loops by two slings, and a cast brass loop sewn on one end to connect to the beltplate. These belts were very little worn (only

33

1,500 were made or bought), most heavy artillerymen receiving the infantryman's waist belt and accoutrements.

Cap boxes

The box which held the copper percussion caps was of black leather, 3 in. long and deep and 1¼ in. wide, with an inner cover with end pieces. A hole on the bottom of the outer flap fastened onto a brass stud. There were two loops riveted to the back through which the waistbelt was slipped. Inside a natural sheepskin strip 1½ in. wide was glued and sewn to the back surface to keep the caps from falling out in action. On the left side was a steel wire cone-pick, 1.5 in. long, with a ½ in. diameter ring handle, carried in a loop. This was used to clean out the musket cone, or nipple, if necessary. Between January 1, 1861, and June 30, 1866, the Army made or bought 376,305 cap boxes, in addition to complete equipment sets.

Co. A, 23rd Massachusetts Inf. wore this modified Zouave uniform with rather narrow trousers, a regulation forage cap, and a jacket plainer than was usual among these units; the trim and sash are sky blue. (Rick Carlile)

A sergeant of the 95th Pennsylvania Vol. Inf. wears his Zouave jacket with ordinary issue trousers and a military-style waistcoat; note, on the left breast of the waistcoat, the VI Corps' Greek cross badge, apparently in a fancy form. (Author's collection)

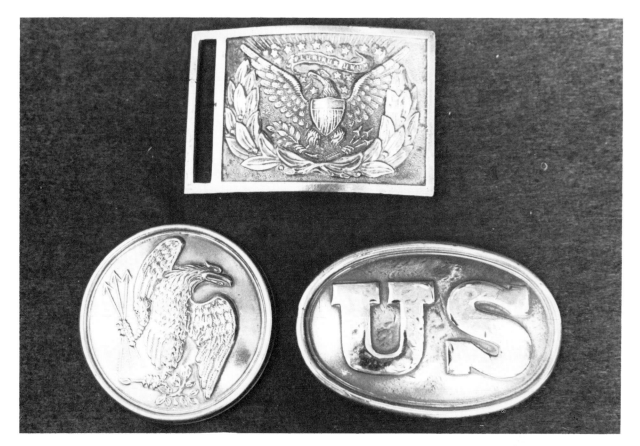

Bayonets and scabbards

The steel socket bayonets used with the Springfield and Enfield rifle-muskets were similar. Both had 18-in. long triangular-section blades and 3-in. sockets. Both mounted to the sight base stud on the top of the musket barrel. The US bayonet blade was $^{25}/_{32}$ in. wide, the British-made blade was $^{13}/_{16}$ in. wide; the US shank was $1^{1}/_{4}$ in. long, and the Enfield type was 1in. long.

The black bridle-leather Springfield bayonet scabbard was $19^{1}/_{2}$ in. long, with a brass chape, and a black buff-leather frog sewn and riveted together and to the scabbard at an angle. The Army acquired 416,290 bayonet scabbards additional to complete equipment sets purchased.

Cartridge Boxes

The cartridge box for the 0.58-in. caliber rifled musket was of heavy black leather, with a light upper-leather inner cover with end pieces sewn to it. One or the other flap was often marked with a maker's name and an Army inspector's mark. A strap sewn and riveted to the flap held the box closed by means of a brass stud. Under the flap, on the box front, was an implement pocket for

Top, the brass beltplate with an applied silver wreath, as worn by officers and non-commissioned officers, and all enlisted men of mounted branches. *Bottom left*, the circular brass plate worn, with different rear fittings, on the enlisted man's cartridge box cross belt and the NCO's sword belt. *Bottom right*, the stamped brass plate, backed with lead, worn on the waist belt by infantry enlisted men. (Author's collection)

musket tools and patches. On the back were two vertical loops so it could be carried on a waist belt, and two horizontal loops for the shoulder belt. An oval stamped brass plate, $3^{1}/_{2}$ in. by 2.2 in. and bearing the letters "US," was centered on the outside of the flap. In late 1864 the Army began having the letters "US" within an oval border stamped into the leather to save metal costs. Inside the box were two tins, each with a lower division, open in front, which held a bundle of ten cartridges; and two upper divisions, one containing six and the other four cartridges. Records show that an additional 190,684 of these boxes were made or bought between January 1, 1861, and June 30, 1866.

The cartridge box could be carried on the waist belt (most Zouaves carried them this way), but only 5.3 percent of regular Army of the Potomac

The issue cap box had the belt loops both sewn and riveted on. Note inspector's mark on the flap; these appeared on most US Army leather accoutrements purchased from private contractors, and each sub-inspector had his own stamp. This one reads **"F.A. SNIFFEN/SUB.INSPECTOR"** in two arcs around **"U.S./ORD.DEPT."** (Author's collection)

infantrymen photographed in the field carry the box on the waist belt. Indeed, II Corps orders said the box was not to "be attached to the waist belt, but must be suspended from the cross belt, resting on the hip."

The carbine cartridge box for most carbines, such as the Sharps, was like the infantry cartridge box except that it had only two vertical belt loops on the back, and was smaller in depth. The army acquired an additional 238,520 of these boxes during the war, and 171,264 of the similar but smaller pistol cartridge box.

Haversacks

The basic issue haversack was made of black painted cotton. It was 12½ in. by 3 ⅓ in. by 13 in., with a 5-in. flap buckled closed by a single leather strap. A tin cup was often slung by the handle on this strap. Inside there was a white cotton bag for carrying food, held in place by three tin buttons. Officially, the flaps were to be marked in white paint with the number and name of the regiment, the company letter, and the soldier's number. These markings were rarely seen in actual field use. According to regulations, the haversack was to be worn on the left side, with the canteen worn over it. The Army bought or made 4,564,608 haversacks between January 1, 1861, and June 30, 1866.

Holsters

Holsters were made of black leather, shaped to be worn on the right but with the butt to the front, with a flap that buttoned to a brass stud covering the

The first model cartridge box for the M1855 and subsequent rifled muskets had a separate brass plate on the outer flap; as an economy measure, the government started to replace this with the same motif simply stamped into the leather from 1864. (Author's collection)

revolver butt. The tab that fastened to the stud was attached to the flap by a copper rivet and a semicircle of stitching. The Army bought or made an additional 325,452 holsters between January 1, 1861, and June 30, 1866.

Canteens

The canteen was a tin oblate spheroid (looking rather like a squashed cannonball!) with a pewter mouthpiece, and three tin loops through which the white cotton carrying strap passed. It was 7.8 in. in diameter, 2½ in. thick in the center, and held almost three pints. It had a cork stopper with a tin cap on top, held by an iron pin passing through the cork and turned into a ring on top, the ring being attached by a chain to one tin carrying strap loop to prevent loss. Some had concentric raised rings stamped into the front and back faces for added strength. The canteen was covered with grey, tan, sky blue, or dark blue wool. Soldiers often wrote their names and unit designations on these covers. The Army bought or made 5,200,614 canteens between January 1, 1861, and June 30, 1866.

Black-painted canvas haversack, fastened with a leather strap and buckle; the soldier used it to carry rations, in a separate cotton inner bag, and sometimes ammunition. The tag tied to the buckle here is a museum identification. (N. Carolina Museum of History)

This issue canteen is covered with dirty tan cloth, on which the original owner marked his name and company letter on both sides. (Author's collection)

Knapsacks

The most common issue knapsacks were of black painted canvas, with two bags attached at the top and strapped together at the bottom. The "front" bag was 13½ in. wide and 14 in. high; the "rear" bag (that was worn against the body) was 11 in. high and 14 in. wide. Three narrow leather straps on the bottom surface buckled tight to close the knapsack. Two leather loops on the top surface were used to hold leather straps for fastening a blanket roll to the top. Two 2-in. wide shoulder straps were sewn to the rear bag; these passed forward over the shoulders, ending in a brass stud which connected to two narrow straps roughly at the front of the shoulder. One of these narrow straps from each shoulder stud passed down, under the arm, and hooked to the rear bag, while the other was designed to hook to the front of the M1855 rifleman's belt. As these belts were very rare, the user usually hooked the narrow straps across the chest into the opposite shoulder strap, or under the waist belt.

Knapsacks were officially to be marked on the back with the regimental number 1½ in. high, in yellow for artillery and white for infantry; inside, the company letter and soldier's number were to be marked, too. These markings were rarely seen after the knapsack's first issue. The Army bought or made 3,583,324 knapsacks between January 1, 1861, and June 30, 1866.

Knapsacks were often not worn on campaign.

Cpl. George Fowle, 39th Massachusetts Infantry, recalled in July 1863 that his unit left their knapsacks behind, and he "carried my overcoat with the cape cut off until Thursday when I left it besides the road. All I carry is a piece of shelter tent, rubber blanket, and the clothes I have on." Such behavior was typical of a unit on the march. Even when the men were not ordered to leave their knapsacks behind, many abandoned them anyway. A 118th Pennsylvania infantryman recalled: "The combrous [sic] knapsack had been abandoned for its less military substitute, and the roll of blanket, gum-blanket, and shelter half found its place...." The 100th Indiana's Pvt. Upson recalled that "all a good many carry is their blanket made into a roll with their rubber 'poncho' which is doubled around and tied at the ends and hung over the left shoulder."

Blankets, shelter-halves and ponchos

The Army bought or made 5,910,059 grey-brown wool and 1,893,007 rubber blankets and 1,596,559 ponchos between January 1, 1861, and June 30, 1866. The wool blankets had the black letters "US" stitched in the center in outline form in letters 4 in. high, with 2¾ in. black stripes at each narrow end. The blankets measured 7ft by 5½ ft, and so were large enough to roll up in.

The rubber blankets and ponchos were made of rubber-coated or black-painted cotton. The difference in the two appears to be that ponchos had a slit 3 in. wide and 16 in. long in the center, and so could be worn over the head as a rain cape, while rubber blankets were plain. Soldiers used both terms for the rubber or "gum" blanket and the poncho interchangeably, and it is not known now if infantrymen received true ponchos or just rubber blankets. Both were 60 in. wide by 71 in. long (a variation is 45 in. by 70 in.), with brass eyelets on the outer edge so that they could be tied over a tent for additional waterproofing. Soldiers often painted the white inner side with checkerboards or "chuck-a-luck" boards.

The shelter-half, which Billings said was never made of "anything heavier than cotton drilling," was 5ft 2 in. long by 4ft 8 in. wide originally, 5 ft 6 in. by 5 ft 5 in. from 1864; with nine tin or zinc buttons on the top edge and seven on the end. There were 23 buttonholes on the upper edge and side; three loops were attached to each end, and it came with a 6 ft 10 in. manila line of six threads. According to Billings, "two muskets with bayonets fixed were stuck erect into the ground the width of a half shelter apart. A guy rope which went with every half shelter was stretched between the trigger-guards of the muskets, and over this ridge pole the tent was pitched in a twinkling." Strong, a soldier of the 105th Illinois, recalled: "Two of the halves buttoned together and stretched over a pole made a shelter from the dew, but not much shelter from the rain. Six of them, the length of two with one at each end, would hold six men by a little crowding."

WEAPONS

Infantry longarms

In a scramble to furnish infantry longarms for all the men who volunteered for service in 1861, the Army obtained weapons from anywhere and everywhere. The élite Iron Brigade of the Army of the Potomac was described in January 1862 as having a mixture of Austrian rifled muskets, Belgian rifled muskets, 0.69-in. caliber Springfield smoothbore muskets that had been converted from flint to percussion, and M1861 Springfield 0.58-in. caliber rifled muskets. In the same year the 69th Pennsylvania Infantry Regiment had P1853 Enfields, M1861 Springfields, and M1842 Springfields. In 1863 the regiment received a bunch of Austrian, Prussian and Saxon rifled muskets. It was not until 1864 that they were all armed with 0.58-in. or 0.577-in. (Enfield caliber) rifled muskets. In the Army of the Tennessee this mixed ammunition

Two slightly differing versions of the P1853 Enfield rifled musket, which was very similar to the US-made rifled musket and was the second most widely used infantry longarm of the war; and (detail) the lockplate of a P1853 made in Birmingham under Northern contract – it does not have the interchangeable parts found on Enfield-made weapons, and is generally rather more crudely finished than was the case with British Army muskets. (Milwaukee Public Museum; and Author's collection)

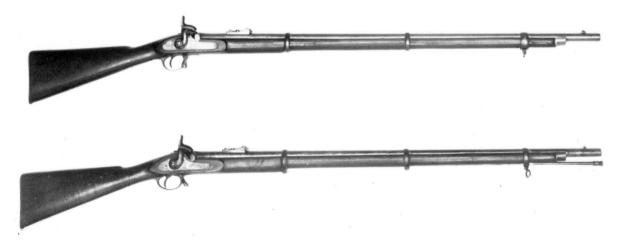

problem was solved on April 21, 1863, when arms were switched about from company to company to ensure a standard caliber within, at least, each company.

The basic infantry longarms included, nevertheless, the M1842 smoothbore 0.69-in. caliber musket made in Springfield, Massachusetts, and Harpers Ferry, Virginia. The Army modernized 14,182 of these weapons between 1856 and 1859, adding rifling and long-range sights.

The M1855 rifled musket, 0.58-in. caliber, was the first rifled musket the Army designed to use the "Minie" ball. It also featured a priming system using a roll of paper percussion caps which were automatically advanced to prime the weapon with each cocking of the hammer. A total of 59,273 of these were made by the Army, while Eli Whitney, Jr., in Connecticut, also made a number under contract.

As the M1855 rifled muskets were expensive to produce, with special long-range sights like those on the P1853 Enfield and iron patch boxes in the stocks, in 1861 the Army introduced a simplified version of this weapon. It had a sight set only to three settings, the furthest being 500 yards, and no automatic primer or patchbox. The M1861 became the standard infantry arm of the US Army during the war, and was produced by government armories and by 22 manufacturers in the US, Belgium, and Germany. A total of 670,617, of which 265,129 were made in Springfield, were made during the war.

In 1863 a few changes were made to the M1861, with the barrel bands now held in position with screws, like the P1853 Enfield, and the cone seat being flattened with the clean-out screw removed. A new S-shaped hammer replaced the older one which had fitted over the patented M1855-type primer. In practice, it was found that the barrel bands worked loose under prolonged firing; and in 1864 they were replaced with clips, and the screws on the bands were removed.

Besides all the American-made weapons, a number of foreign weapons were imported. The most popular of these was the long British P1853 Enfield rifled musket, of which 428,292 were bought for Union troops, becoming the second standard infantry longarm. The M1854 Austrian 0.54-in. Lorenz rifled musket was also popular, with some 226,294 of them being imported for the Army. The Army also imported 141,570 Prussian muskets, 57,467 Belgian rifles, and 44,250 French rifles.

The Colt "Navy" .36-in. revolver, the most popular officer's weapon of the period. (Author's collection)

While all these standard muzzle-loaders were being produced, technology was available for the production of breech-loaders, which would have been preferred by many infantrymen in the field. Ordnance, however, feared that their introduction would simply lead to a waste of ammunition. (Moreover, they were much more expensive than the $13 M1861 Springfield.) Still, many infantrymen did get breech-loaders. One of the most popular was the Sharps M1859 0.52-in. caliber rifle, which used a sliding breechblock opened by swinging the trigger guard down, with a standard percussion cap and hammer. The Army bought 9,141 of these weapons.

The Spencer rifle was more advanced, however, as it used a 0.52-in. caliber ball fixed in a brass cartridge that contained its own primer; the rifle thus represented a whole new generation of weapons. These cartridges were loaded into a magazine tube that ran from the rear of the stock to the breech. The commander of Wilder's "Lightning Brigade" wrote that his unit had "repeatedly routed and driven largely superior forces of rebels, in some instances five or six times our number, and this result is mainly due to our being armed with the Spencer repeating rifle." Even with this endorsement, the Army bought only 12,471 Spencers during the war.

Another breech-loader that used brass cartridges was the Henry. It was the ancestor of the famous Winchester that "won the West," and looked much like it, except that the breech was brass and there was no wooden forestock. A 100th Indiana private wrote that he had bought a Henry from a wounded 97th Indiana soldier in May 1864, to replace his issued muzzle-loader, for $35: a sum which shows what value he placed on the weapon, when one considers his salary of $13 a month. "I am glad I could get it," he wrote home. "They are good shooters and I like to think I have so many shots in reserve." Once again, despite such endorsements, the Army bought only 1,731 Henry rifles out of a war-time production of some 10,000.

The issue sling for all infantry longarms was russet brown leather, 1.15 in. wide and 46 in. long. It had a brass hook at one end fastened to the sling with two brass rivets, and a leather loop at the other. They were usually marked with a maker's name or inspector's mark. The Army bought or made 265,866 of these between January 1, 1861, and June 30, 1866 – clearly, not nearly enough for every rifled musket it made or bought.

Some indication of what proportion of soldiers had slings on their weapons can be gained, for example, by the ordnance return of Co. B, 72nd Pennsylvania Volunteer Infantry Regiment, dated March 31, 1863. The company had 20 Springfield rifled muskets, 17 Enfield rifled muskets, four Belgian rifles, and one Austrian rifled musket – a total of 42 longarms. However, while they had a full set of accoutrements for each soldier, there were only 15 gun slings in the whole company. (There were, in addition, four ball screws, used in removing unfired ammunition from the bore; one spring vice, used in taking the lock parts apart; 15 screwdrivers; six wipers, used in holding swabs when cleaning the musket bores with the ramrods; and 20 tompions, wooden plugs used to keep the bore clean when not in use.)

Cavalry longarms

The longarm of the cavalryman was the carbine, a weapon which came in an astonishing variety of

This Colt "Army" .45-in. revolver was carried by Maj. A. W. Corliss of 7th Sqn., Rhode Island Cavalry. (Chris Nelson collection)

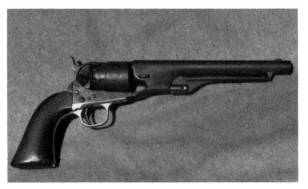

models. The only official model was the US pistol-carbine, M1855. This was simply a muzzle-loading, 0.58-in. caliber pistol, made much like the M1855 rifled musket, but with a handstock and, obviously, a shorter barrel. With it came a detachable stock that could be mounted on to it to make a carbine. The pistol was carried in one holster, and the stock in another, on the saddle. Some 8,000 of these weapons were made before the war began, and issued to the regular army cavalry regiments. They were rare among volunteer units.

The most popular volunteer carbine was probably the Spencer breech-loader. Like the Spencer infantry rifle, it used a brass cartridge containing powder, bullet, and primer, and was loaded with a tubular magazine through the butt. Over 110,500 Spencer carbines were bought by the Army after its introduction and before the war's end. Its dependability and high rate of fire earned it high praise. One major wrote in May 1864: "We could have held our position against any force brought before it, for with the Spencer carbine, plenty of ammunition, and a determined set of men, nothing can stand before them."

Another popular weapon, though not a repeater, was the Sharps breech-loading M1859 or M1863 carbine. Some 50,000 of both models were bought by the Army during the war. They were of 0.52-in. caliber, with a falling breech, and were loaded individually with linen cartridges. The first models had brass barrel bands, trigger guards and butt plates, but these were made of iron on the 1863 model.

The Burnside breech-loading carbine used a brass cartridge, but also required a separate percussion cap: the cartridge was simply designed to prevent a flash through the gap between the receiver and breech. There were four models of Burnside carbines, all of which were of 0.54-in. carbine; the second model had an improved breech locking system, the third had a wooden forestock and steel barrel band, and the fourth was shorter and had a sling swivel and blued steel finish. Between all four models, the Army bought 55,500 of these weapons.

The Army also bought 30,300 Smith carbines, a 0.50-in. caliber breech-loader which used India-rubber or metallic foil cartridges. These were inserted into a breech that opened by "breaking" the weapon like a modern shotgun. The historian of the 1st Massachusetts Cavalry said that they were

"not a good weapon" and that they were disliked in his regiment. Part of the problem was that dirt particles around the breech could cause a flash in the firer's face after a number of shots.

In addition to these main examples, a large variety of carbines made by private manufacturers to their own designs were bought by the Army in smaller quantities. Among these were the Gallagher (22,728 bought), the Starr (20,600), the Maynard (20,002), the Remington (20,000), the Merrill (14,495), the Joslyn (11,261), the Cosmopolitan (9,342), the Warner (4,001), the Ballard (1,509), the Gibbs (1,052), the Ball (1,002), the Palmer (1,001), the Lindner (892), and the Wesson (151).

The issue carbine belt was of black buff or bridle leather, 56 in. long and 2.5 in. wide. It had a brass buckle and tip, with a bright iron swivel and "D" ring with a roller 2.62 in. long. Between January 1, 1861, and June 30, 1866, 236,398 carbine belts were acquired, in addition to complete sets.

Handguns

As with carbines, there was no official model of handgun, nor did the Army make its own, depending instead on private contractors.

Three US Army cavalry carbines: *top*, Smith carbine carried by Sgt. Franklin I. Thomas, Co. A, 12th Illinois Cav. – the catch in front of the trigger allowed it to be "broken" for reloading like a shotgun; *center*, Spencer repeater carried by Sgt. Bowers, 9th Indiana Cav; and *bottom*, Sharps carried by Sgt. Cannaday, 2nd Pennsylvania Cav. (Chris Nelson collection)

Throughout the war the Army bought some 374,000 revolvers for its officers and mounted men.

Revolvers came basically in two sizes, the "Army" of 0.44-in. caliber and the "Navy" of 0.36-in. caliber. The designations do not indicate that soldiers used only "Army" revolvers: indeed, the handier so-called "Navy" category was the more popular size among officers who bought their own weapons.

The most common revolver was made by Samuel Colt. It was six-shot, single-action, using self-consuming cartridges and separate percussion caps; it had walnut grips, a brass trigger guard, and all hardened steel cylinder, frame, and barrel. The Army bought 129,730 "Army" revolvers and 17,110 M1851 and M1861 "Navy" revolvers from Colt during the war. The revolvers had notched frames which accepted a detachable shoulder stock, but this feature was little used in practice.

The second most important revolver in terms of numbers was made by E. Remington and Sons. These weapons, which again came both in "Army" and "Navy" models, differed from Colts in that they had a steel strap across the top of the cylinder for added strength. Remington produced about 5,000 M1861 "Army" revolvers and some 5,000 "Navy" revolvers in 1862.

The Army bought 11,284 Savage "Navy" revolvers between late 1861 and June 1862; these were unusual in that they had two triggers – the bottom one rotated the cylinder and cocked the weapon, and the top one fired it. They were unpopular, and were not often seen later in the war. Starr produced some 23,000 M1858 and 31,000 M1862 "Army" revolvers for the US Army. The first models were double-action, but the second models, in response to complaints from the field, were single-action. Starr also produced some 3,000 M1860 "Navy" revolvers, of which 1,402 were sold to the US government. Whitney made a "Navy" revolver with a strap over the cylinder like the Remington design; of some 32,000 manufactured, 14,000 were sold to the US Government. The government also bought 198 Allen & Wheelock M1858 "Army" revolvers; 1,100 Joslyn M1858 "Army" five-shot revolvers; and 2,001 Pettengill M1858 "Army" double-action, hammerless revolvers made by Rogers & Spencer. They also imported quantities of revolvers, including 12,374 French-made Lefaucheux weapons.

Edged weapons
Between January 1, 1861, and June 30, 1866, the Army bought 203,285 light cavalry sabers, 189,114 heavy cavalry sabers, 20,751 horse artillery sabers, 797 staff officers' swords, 1,279 cavalry officers' sabers, 2,038 foot officers' swords, 86,655 non-commissioned officers' swords, 33,531 musicians' swords, 2,152 foot artillery swords (clearly far too few to actually equip all foot artillery personnel), 300 cutlasses, and 4,301 lances (which were carried by the 6th Pennsylvania Cavalry Regiment and some smaller commands until 1863, when the lance was placed in store).

The 41-in. light cavalry saber was first made in 1857, with a curved blade 1 in. wide at the hilt, a brass half-basket guard, Phrygian helmet pattern pommel, and black leather-wrapped grips bound with twisted brass wire with a swell in the center. It was marked, as were all the Army's swords, at the top of the blade with the maker's name, date, and inspector's initials. The M1840 heavy cavalry saber was quite similar, but with a blade an inch and a quarter wide at the hilt, and with no swell in the grips. Both had iron scabbards with two rings. Officers used the same sabers but with floral designs cast into the hilt.

The M1840 horse artillery saber had a sharply curved blade with a single brass branch guard and Phrygian helmet pommel. The grips were like those of the cavalry saber. These weapons were disliked; but then again, as there were 13,811 more light artillerymen than there were sabers for them, it is not surprising that the large majority of photographed light artillerymen, if they carry sabers at all (and few do), carry light cavalry rather than artillery weapons. Officers used the same sabers with etched blades.

The saber knot for all enlisted men's sabers was of dark brown bridle or buff leather, 1 in. wide and 36 in. long, with one end of the strap fastened to a 3-in. tassel; the other end was passed through the tassel after going around the saber guard, and was fastened by one of the tassel tags. During the war years the Army bought 225,975 of them.

The M1833 foot artillery sword was even less used than the horse artillery saber. It had a cast brass hilt with an eagle on the trilobate pommel and scales on the grip. The blade was 1fl in. wide at the hilt, and 25¼ in. long overall.

The M1840 non-commissioned officer's sword had a straight 38½-in. blade and a cast brass hilt with a round pommel, a single branch, and imitation wire grips. Scabbards were leather with brass throats and chapes, although japanned black iron examples were sometimes issued. The M1840 musician's sword was virtually the same as the NCO sword, but was about 3¼ in. shorter and lacked counter-guards.

The M1850 staff and field officer's sword had a slightly curved blade just over 1 in. wide at the hilt. It was etched with military and floral designs and the national eagle. Similar designs and the letters "US" were cast into the hilt. The scabbard was bright or browned iron. The M1860 staff and field Officer's sword had a straight blade with an eagle and shield on the brass pommel, and a nickled steel scabbard.

The M1850 foot officer's sword was the common infantry officer's sword. It had a slightly curved blade just over an inch wide at the hilt, which was engraved, and a brass hilt with fishskin-wrapped grips bound with twisted brass wire. Overall length was around 36 in. Scabbards were black leather of japanned iron.

THE PLATES

A1: Colonel, Infantry, 1861
This colonel wears the field-grade officer's full dress, with dress hat, frock coat, and the 1861 dark trousers. His regimental number appears on each epaulet, on a circle of sky blue, the infantry branch-of-service color. His sword is the foot officer's sword.

A2: Sergeant major, Infantry, 1861
This sergeant major wears the enlisted man's version of the regulation full dress uniform, with a non-commissioned officer's sword, and staff non-commissioned officer's brass shoulder scales, Note also the national color of the 13th Illinois Infantry Regiment, which was to be captured by Confederate troops and kept in Richmond, Virginia. Found there when the city fell in 1865, it was the first US color to fly over that city since Virginia left the Union in 1861. It is generally representative of all US infantry regimental national colors, although those carried by troops of some states differed slightly – e.g. those carried by Pennsylvania infantry units had the state seal painted or embroidered in the canton with the stars surrounding it. (Inscription: "13th ILL.")

A3: First lieutenant, Infantry, 1861
In the field, many officers continued wearing the frock coat, but with shoulder straps instead of epaulets. This man wears the regulation officer's sword belt, and a pre-war style cap box with a shield-type flap in front.

The typical company-grade officer's uniform in the field displayed by this group from the 1st Connecticut Artillery, photographed near Yorktown, Virginia, in early 1862. The man in the center rear has an oilcloth cover on his cap; there is a mixture of dark and sky blue trousers, worn over or inside boots; and a mixture of forage caps, of both regular and "McClellan" shape, slouch hats and dress hats. (US Army Mil. Hist. Inst.)

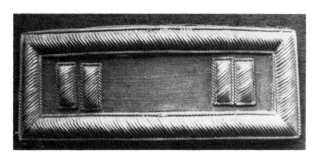

An infantry captain's shoulder strap; the backing is sky blue cotton, the border and rank bars are stamped metal made to resemble embroidery. The bars are only pinned in place – many officers simply pinned them directly to shoulder or collar, making them less conspicuous in action. This example bears a patent date of June 18, 1861. (Author's collection)

B1: Lieutenant-colonel, Cavalry, 1863

Mounted officers wore the regulation frock coat, as does this lieutenant-colonel. Branch-of-service color formed the background for the shoulder straps, here in cavalry yellow. His cap has the pointed, narrow peak popular with many officers. He is armed with a cavalry officer's saber embellished with a metallic gold thread officer's saber knot – an item more generally carried by cavalry officers than by those in other branches of service. Note here the rear cut of the officer's frock coat.

B2: Sergeant, Cavalry, 1863

Many cavalrymen preferred to wear the dress jacket, without shoulder scales, in the field. This NCO's fatigue cap has a branch-of-service badge, not generally worn by infantrymen but common in the cavalry. On his belt he carries – reading around from the right front hip – his cap box, holster, pistol cartridge box, and carbine cartridge box.

This cavalry sergeant holds a guidon of the type used from 1863. The earlier type was of the same dimensions, but halved red over white. The letters "US" and the troop letter appeared on the top half in white, and the regimental number on the bottom half, in red.

B3: Captain, Cavalry, 1863

The short, plain jacket was preferred by mounted officers to the frock coat for field use. It was worn with one or two rows of buttons by company grade or field grade officers respectively. This figure also displays the low, stylish "McClellan" or "Chasseur" style cap so popular with officers. Typical of many officers in the field, he wears plain issue enlisted man's trousers.

C1: Captain, Light Artillery, 1864

The black slouch hat, although not regulation, was one of the most popular forms of headgear among both officers and men, especially those of the mounted branches. The short mounted man's jacket worn by light artillery officers featured the "Russian" shoulder knot with the silver insignia of rank at the outer end. Company grade officers used this relatively simple shoulder knot, with one, two, or three rows of braid according to rank. Field grade officers wore four rows of braid in a somewhat more elaborate but basically similar design.

Regulation buttons: *top*, artillery and infantry officers'; *center*, rifle officer's, and enlisted man's; *bottom*, waistcoat or cuff buttons of a cavalry officer and an enlisted man. (Author's collection)

A mortar crew practice in a seacoast installation. Note variety of dark and light blue trousers. The two officers at right wear respectively a slouch hat and frock coat, and a forage cap and fatigue blouse. The left-hand front man of the four carrying the shell in the "callipers" wears the large leather gunner's haversack. (US Army Mil. Hist. Inst.)

C2: Corporal, Light Artillery, 1864

The full dress of the light artillery included this dress shako which was, in practice, very little worn. This corporal is a veteran, as indicated by the service stripe worn above each cuff. The artillery wore their stripes edged in sky blue when showing wartime service, as all other branches had the stripes edged in red. His saber is actually a cavalry model rather than the unpopular and relatively rare light artillery saber. The guidon is that of the 19th Independent Battery, Ohio Veteran Volunteer Artillery, and is typical of light artillery guidons. The 19th served with Sherman from the Cumberland Gap to Atlanta; at the defense of Nashville; and finally at Durham Station, North Carolina. The unit received 29 battle honors by the end of the war, some of which have already been marked on this color.

C3: Regimental quartermaster sergeant, Heavy Artillery, 1864

This regimental quartermaster sergeant wears the full dress uniform of the heavy artillery branch, including the rarely seen M1833 foot artillery sword, a Romanesque fantasy inspired by the French M1831 "cabbage-cutter." His shoulder scales are actually the sergeant's models, rather than the riveted staff pattern he should wear, indicating recent promotion.

A mortar crew practice in a seacoast installation. Note variety of dark and light blue trousers. The two officers at right wear respectively a slouch hat and frock coat, and a forage cap and fatigue blouse. The left-hand front man of the four carrying the shell in the "callipers" wears the large leather gunner's haversack. (US Army Mil. Hist. Inst.)

D1: Private, Infantry, 1863

This is the man who fought all the battles, who took most of the losses, and bore the brunt of fighting: a soldier of the infantry, the branch which the US Army calls the "Queen of Battles." This is how he generally looked in the field. He is little burdened with parade ground fancies, or much embellished with insignia. (He does, however, wear the issue knapsack, while many of his friends have lost or thrown theirs away by now.)

D2: Second lieutenant, Infantry, 1863

In the field, officers dressed little better than their men. This lieutenant has a privately made copy of the issue fatigue blouse. His slouch hat bears the badge of the 1st Division, V Corps. His haversack, privately bought, is of leather, with a removable unpainted canvas bag for food inside. His leather canteen has a pewter spout and copper rivets and is lined with tinfoil: it was patented in 1862, and is a surprisingly commonly found relic.

D3: First (orderly) sergeant, Infantry, 1863

Many soldiers, given their choice, wore the dress frock coat in the field instead of the blouse. It is seen here from the rear, with its tell-tale buttons on the waistline. This sergeant holds the regimental, or second, color of the 60th Ohio Volunteer Infantry Regiment, which matches the regulation regimental color quite closely. The 60th served in the IX Corps in the 1864 campaign of the Army of the Potomac, from the Wilderness to the capture of Petersburg. (Lower riband "60TH REG'T O.V.I.")

E1: Company quartermaster sergeant, Cavalry, 1864

Although it was not regulation until 1866, the single "tie" over the chevrons of the company quartermaster sergeant appears in many photographs taken of soldiers as early as 1863. This one wears a popular cavalryman's item, the plain blue "roundabout" or "shell" jacket, with veteran's service stripes above his cuffs. His regimental number is worn on his cap top. His carbine is a Spencer repeater, and he carries the associated Blakeslee Quickloader cartridge box; this had a sling, and a loop low down for securing it to the saber belt, and held ten tubular seven-round Spencer magazines. The Army bought 32,000 of them between 1862 and June 1866.

E2: Private, 1st Division, IV Corps, 1864

This private wears his regulation corps badge on his cap top. He has the issue grey flannel shirt and wears his trousers, as was most common, without braces. He holds a tin coffee boiler's cup, a piece of campaigning kit considered vital by every man: from a morale standpoint, coffee was probably the most important single ration issue item.

E3: Musician, Cavalry, 1864

All musicians were marked by the stripes and frame of branch-of-service color braid worn on their chests. This man holds an issue bugle with a branch-of-service color cord and tassels; riflemen often used green cords and tassels, while artillerymen had red. He has both a regimental number and a company letter on his cap top.

F1: Private, Infantry, 1862

The Army imported 10,000 of the French Army's Chasseur uniforms and issued them to a number of infantry units (see details in body of text). Many of them had to be let out in the seams, as the Americans who wore them tended to be bigger than the French for whom they had been made. This man wears the issue *bonnet de police*; a shako was also issued for dress occasions.

F2: Private, 35th New Jersey Infantry, 1864

The Zouave uniform, as seen from the back, shows the cartridge box protruding from under the jacket: many units wore the boxes on their waist belts, but the 35th wore theirs on shoulder belts worn under the jackets. The 35th also originally wore dark blue képis trimmed with yellow, these being replaced with fezzes in 1864. The regiment was initially armed with P1853 Enfield rifled muskets, although these were later replaced with Springfields. This man already wears the Springfield bayonet scabbard. The regiment served in Sherman's XXII Corps in Georgia and the Carolinas.

F3: Private, 5th New York Infantry, 1863

The Zouave uniform worn by the 5th New York was probably the example most closely resembling that of the actual French Zouaves. A state beltplate was worn, although the cartridge box plate was the issue US item. The 5th took quite a beating at the hands

A pair of US Army foot soldier's boots, noticeably square-toed, with four lace holes each side; they were often made with the flesh side of the leather outwards. (Smithsonian Inst.)

of the Texas Brigade, both in the Peninsular Campaign and at Second Bull Run, never regaining its former fame after the latter battle.

G1: Private, 155th Pennsylvania Infantry, 1864

Zouave uniforms were issued to this unit as a mark of its abilities at drill several years after the unit was first raised. The regiment wore its 1st Division, V Corps badges on their jacket fronts, making a part of the decoration. He is armed with an M1863 Springfield rifled musket.

G2: Captain, 155th Pennsylvania Infantry, 1864

Zouave officers did not wear the same uniforms as their men. In many units they were only distinguished by colorful képis and, perhaps, gaiters. In the 155th, however, there were several variations of Zouave officer dress, of which this was the most common.

G3: Private, 3rd Division, XIII Corps, 1864

Some Western regiments adopted parts of Zouave dress, but usually nothing as elaborate as that worn by Eastern units. This simplified, "semi-Zouave" jacket was peculiar to men of the 3rd Division, XIII Corps, such as the 34th Indiana Infantry. It is typical of jackets worn by men from Ohio, Illinois, Indiana, and other Western states.

H1: Musician, 3rd Division, II Corps, 1865

The foot soldier's overcoat, as worn by this drummer, was a popular piece of uniform. He wears a corps badge on his cap in divisional color. His drum is of the regulation design. The basic eagle and riband design, similar to that which appeared on regimental colors, was the same for all branches of service, but the field for artillery was red instead of the infantry's blue. The drum is slung on an issue white web sling. Orders in the field were often still passed by drum; drum calls also regulated the soldier's daily timetable in camp.

H2: Private, Light Artillery, 1865

This soldier, armed with a light artillery saber, wears

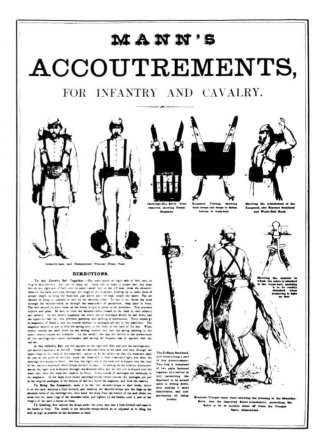

This information sheet shows an improved system of leather accoutrements patented in December 1863 by William D. Mann. The Army bought 37,000 sets of infantry equipment and 12,020 sets of the cavalry version. These were mostly used for testing during the Civil War, and were never adopted by the Army as a whole. (Author's collection)

the mounted man's overcoat, with its two rows of buttons and longer cape. He has a government-made brown leather gunner's haversack. This was used to carry ammunition from the limber chest to the piece when in action, thus protecting the flannel bags of powder from sparks.

H3: Major, Heavy Artillery, 1865

The officer's overcoat was dark blue, with black silk braids on the cuff indicating rank: this major's rank is shown by the three rows of braid. He wears a lower-type dress hat known as a "Burnside" or "Kossuth" hat, which was quite popular among officers of the period.

INDEX

(References to illustrations are shown in **bold**. Plates are shown with page and caption indicators in brackets.)